The Hammer Horror Encyclopedia

Brian Carver

Contents

Introduction

British film company Hammer Films produced a wide selection of popular films from 1937 to 1979. The studio is principally known for its horror films made from the 1950s-1970s.

Hammer Horror films were extremely popular. They were – and still are - well regarded, and innovative with many new artistic elements and increasingly adult and violent content.

Hammer Horror films had many iconic stars such as Sir Christopher Lee and Peter Cushing; the glamorous women of Hammer Horror were a staple.

Find out more about the Hammer Horror series with this book.

The Encyclopedia

A

The Abominable Snowman

The Abominable Snowman (1957)

Directed by Val Guest

Produced by Aubrey Baring

Written by Nigel Kneale

Starring:

Forrest Tucker as Tom Friend, Peter Cushing as Dr. Rollason, Arnold Marlé as The Lhama, Maureen Connell as Helen Rollason

Dr John Rollason, his assistant Peter Fox (Richard Wattis) and Rollason's wife Helen are on a botanical expedition to the Himalayas. They are guests of the Lama at the monastery of Rong-buk.

Another expedition led by Dr. Tom Friend arrives at the monastery. They are searching for the Yeti - the Abominable Snowman. Dr. Rollason decides to join the search for the Yeti.

The film was written by Nigel Kneale and is based on his BBC television play The Creature.

This is a very good early Hammer horror/sci-fi film. It has an unsettling atmosphere and explores issues such as science v commercialism. In the film one explorer wants to study the Yeti, and another wants to make money off the creature.

Aliens

Aliens and extra terrestrials did not really feature much in the Hammer horror series. There was more emphasis on creatures, monsters and magic.

The Quatermass trilogy - The Quatermass Xperiment (1955), Quatermass 2 (1957), Quatermass and the Pit (1967) do feature alien lifeforms and viruses.

Jack Asher

Jack Asher (1916-1991) was a cinematographer.

He worked on several classic Hammer horror films, starting with The Curse of Frankenstein.

Asher had a creative approach to his style of filming with different types of lighting techniques and unique colours. This gave a distinctive look to the Hammer films. He was replaced by Hammer in the early 1960s as his technique was considered too expensive and slow.

B

Don Banks

Don Banks (1923-1980) was an Australian composer.

He composed the music for several Hammer horror films such as Captain Clegg (1962), The Evil of Frankenstein (1964), The Reptile (1966) and The Mummy's Shroud (1967).

Banks was born in Melbourne.

After serving in WW2 he moved to London composing music for advertisements, cartoons, film and television. His Hammer scores complimented the Hammer horror sound with dissonant eerie music.

"Don was a twelve-tone/serial composer who revelled in the opportunity to write abrasive and highly dissonant scores in an idiom akin to that of the late Schoenberg," said composer Douglas Gamley.

In 1972 he returned to Australia to take on educational roles.

Ralph Bates

Ralph Bates (1940-1992) was a British actor.

He appears in Hammer horror films Taste the Blood of

Dracula (1969), The Horror of Frankenstein (1970), Lust for a Vampire (1971), Dr. Jekyll and Sister Hyde (1971) and Fear in the Night (1972).

In Taste the Blood of Dracula he plays Lord Courtley - a dabbler in the occult who turns into Dracula (played by Christopher Lee) after a ceremony. In The Horror of Frankenstein bates plays the main character - Baron Victor Frankenstein. In Lust for a Vampire he plays Giles Garton. In Dr. Jekyll and Sister Hyde he plays Dr. Henry Jekyll, the main character.

He was of French ancestry. Born in Bristol, Bates studied at Trinity College Dublin and Yale Drama School. He had numerous theatre roles, especially early on in his career.

His dark looks led him to be cast in many villainous roles.

Bates appears in many television roles such as Poldark, Moonbase 3, Secret Army and the Minder television film Minder on the Orient Express. He had a memorable role in the John Sullivan BBC sitcom Dear John in the 1980s. He played the title character, a recently divorced man attending a support group for single people.

Bates's second wife was Hammer film actress Virginia Wetherill. They were married until Bates's sad death at 51 from cancer.

James Bernard

James Bernard (1925-2001) was a British film composer. Bernard was born in India, the son of a British Army officer.

During WW2 Bernard worked on deciphering the German Enigma Machine, deciphering Japanese messages. After WW2 Bernard studied at the Royal College of Music. He worked with Benjamin Britten. He was friends with writer Paul Dehn and helped him write a screenplay for Seven Days to Noon (1950) and they won a joint Academy Award for Best Screenplay.

Bernard wrote music for radio and television, and was asked to score the Hammer film The Quatermass Xperiment (1955) when the original composer had to pull out. This was the first of many Hammer films Bernard scored for Hammer. He was responsible for the traditional unsettling and eerie music of the Hammer films.

Bernard died in 2001.

Black Park

Black Park is a country park in Wexham in Buckinghamshire. It is near Pinewood Studios.
The park was used by Hammer as a filming location as it has a lake, dirt tracks and thick woodland, useful for Hammers Gothic period pieces.

Many other films - such as James Bond, Harry Potter, the Marvel Studios films - have used the park as a location.

Blood

Hammer was the first studio to make a horror film showing blood. The Curse of Frankenstein had blood in colour with scenes including blood pouring out of wounds. This was very shocking to audiences in the 50s/60s. Subsequent Hammer films featured lots of blood - which was normally bright red!

Blood From the Mummy's Tomb

Blood From the Mummy's Tomb (1971)

Directed by Seth Holt and Michael Carreras

Produced by Howard Brandy

Written by Christopher Wicking

Starring:

Andrew Keir as Julian Fuchs, Valerie Leon as Margaret Fuchs/Queen Tera, James Villiers as Corbeck, Hugh Burden as Geoffrey Dandridge

Professor Fuchs finds the tomb of evil Egyptian Queen Tara during an expedition in Egypt. He takes her mummy and possessions back to England and recreates her tomb under his house. Fuch's daughter Margaret is given Queen Tara's ring as a birthday gift, and Margaret then has nightmare about the expedition. She is possessed by the spirit of Tara - and wants to gain revenge on the expedition members.

This is the fourth and last film in Hammer's mummy series. It is adapted from Bram Stoker's novel The Jewel of the Seven Stars. Andrew Keir was a late replacement for Peter Cushing who had to pull out as he was suffering from emphysema. Sadly director Seth Holt died of a heart near the end of shooting the film. He was replaced with Michael Carreras.

Blood From the Mummy's Tomb is a stylish 70s Hammer horror. It is helped considerably by the presence of the extremely glamorous Valerie Leon who has a larger than usual role for her. It's a shame that Peter Cushing could not appear due to ill health.

Bray Studios

In 1951 Hammer leased Down Place, a detached house with grounds by the River Thames in Bray in Berkshire. Hammer wanted a place to film without having to lease different country houses. Hammer created the Bray studio's complex using all the rooms and grounds for their films. Hammer sold the studio in 1970.

The studios were used until 2012, and will be converted into housing in the future.

Shane Briant

Shane Briant (1946-2021) was a British actor.

He appears in three Hammer films: Demons of the Mind (1972), Frankenstein and the Monster from Hell (1974) and Captain Kronos - Vampire Hunter (1974)

In Demons of the Minds he plays Emil, one of the young people imprisoned by their father. In Frankenstein and the Monster from Hell he plays Dr. Simon Helder, Dr Frankenstein's assistant. In Captain Kronos - Vampire Hunter he plays Paul Durward.

Born in London, Briant studied law at Trinity College Dublin. After an early career in theatre he had numerous roles in British film and television in the seventies. He was in demand for his classic villainous upper class look.

He moved to Australia in 1983, working in film and television. He wrote several novels.

The Brides of Dracula

The Brides of Dracula (1960)

Directed by Terence Fisher

Produced by Anthony Hinds

Written by Peter Bryan, Edward Percy, Jimmy Sangster and Anthony Hinds.

Starring:

Peter Cushing as Doctor Van Helsing, Marita Hunt as Baroness Meinster, Yvonne Monlaur as Marianne, Freda Jackson as Greta.

A young teacher from France- Marianne Danielle - takes up a post in Transylvania. She stops off at the castle of Baroness Meinster, but is horrified to find his son chained up. She frees him, but her act has unleashed the vampires.

The Brides of Dracula is a sequel to Deacula (1958). Dracula does not appear in the film as Christopher Lee is not in the film. Peter Cushing stars as Van Helsing.

A classic Hammer horror with great production values and performances, especially from Peter Cushing as Van Helsing.

C

Captain Kronos – Vampire Hunter

Captain Kronos – Vampire Hunter (1974)

Directed by Brian Clemens

Produced by Albert Fennell and Brian Clemens

Written by Brian Clemens

Starring:

Horst Janson as Captain Kronos, John Cater as Professor Hieronymus Grost, Caroline Munro as Carla, John Carson as Dr. Marcus

Kronos is a vampire hunter who finds a village with some

woman who have aged prematurely because of a vampire bite. Kronos hunts down the vampires.

The film was actually made in 1972, and not released until 1974. This was the only film directed by British film and television writer and producer Clemens, who worked on many of The Avengers episodes amongst other work. It was going to be the first in a series of Kronos films, but sadly only this one was made.

Another vampire film from Hammer, which is slightly different with the wonderful swashbuckling Captain Kronos character. It's funny and fast paced with lots of action. Also in the cast is the 70s glamour icon Caroline Munro. A cult classic.

James Carreras

Sir James Carreras (1909-1990) was a film producer.

Carreras founded Hammer Films in the 1946 after the original Hammer Films went bankrupt in 1937. From 1949 to 1980 he the Chairman of Hammer Film Productions. His son was Michael Carreras who worked at Hammer as a producer and director.

Michael Carreras

Michael Carreras (1927-1994) was a film producer and director.

He produced numerous films for Hammer.

He also directed The Curse of the Mummy's Tomb (1964) and directed some of Blood from the Mummy's Tomb (1971) after the director passed away during filming. He wrote the screenplay for The Curse of the Mummy's Tomb (1964) under the pen name Michael Younger.

He is the son of Hammer studios founder James Carreras.

John Carson

John Carson (1927-2016) was a British actor.

He appears in three Hammer horror films: The Plague of the Zombies (1966), Taste the Blood of Dracula (1970), Captain Kronos – Vampire Hunter (1974).

In The Plague of the Zombies he plays Squire Clive Hamilton, the villain. In Taste the Blood of Dracula he plays Jonathon Secker, one of the gentlemen who brings Dracula back to life. In Captain Kronos – Vampire Hunter he plays Dr Marcus, a friend of the hero Kronos.

Carson was born in Ceylon (Sri Lanka) to British parents. He was educated in Australia and studied law at Oxford. Early in his career he worked in the theatre.

He had many film and television roles. He was a very versatile actor in demand because of his striking looks and distinctive husky voice which he used to good effect in his Hammer films.

Carson was still remembered as a cult actor late in his life.

He moved to South Africa in the 1980s, and died there in 2016.

Countess Dracula

Countess Dracula (1971)

Directed by Peter Sasdy

Produced by Alexander Paal

Written by Jeremy Paul

Starring:

Ingrid Pitt as Countess Elisabeth Nadasdy (Voice dubbed by Olive Gregg, uncredited), Nigel Green as Captain Dobi, the castle steward, Sandor Elès as Lt. Imre Toth, Maurice Denham as Grand Master Fabio, castle historian

In medieval Europe Countess Elisabeth finds that washing herself in the blood of virgin young girls makes her young again. Her husband Captain Dobi helps to find the girls.

The film is based on the legend of Elizabeth Báthory.

A very lurid story! This is a good typically seventies Hammer horror with some nudity and extra gore. The title is a bit of a cheat as there are no vampires in the film. Horror icon Pitt is great in her role.

The Curse of Frankenstein

The Curse of Frankenstein (1957)

Directed by Terence Fisher
Produced by Anthony Hinds

Written by Jimmy Sangster

Starring:

Peter Cushing as Baron Victor Von Frankenstein,
Christopher Lee as The Creature, Hazel Court as
Elizabeth, Robert Urquart as Dr Paul Krempe

Victor Frankenstein is in prison after being sentenced to
death. He tells his story of how he created a creature to a
priest.

This is the first in Hammer's Frankenstein series which
consisted of seven films. This was Hammer's first colour
horror, and started off their famous series of Gothic
horrors which influenced many other filmmakers. Bernard
Bresslaw was considered for the creature because of his
height. The 6 feet 5 Christopher Lee was finally cast.
Hammer had to make their monster look different from the
iconic look of the Universal Frankenstein film monster.
The Curse of Frankenstein was a big box office hit paving
the way for the numerous Hammer films that followed.

The film is - of course - a classic Hammer horror. It has
the usual wonderful music and artistic visuals, and the
usual great performance by Peter Cushing.

Bray Studios

The Curse of the Mummy's Tomb

The Curse of the Mummy's Tomb (1964)

Directed by Michael Carreras

Produced by Michael Carreras

Written by Henry Younger (Michael Carreras)

Starring:

Terence Morgan as Adam Beauchamp, Ronald Howard as John Bray, Fred Clark as Alexander King, Jeanne Roland as Annette Dubois

Egyptologists find the tomb of the Egyptian Prince Ra. Businessman Alexander King ships the treasures and mummy back to England. But in England someone knows how to bring the mummy back to life.

This is the second of four Hammer mummy films. Trade Union rules stopped one person being credited as director, producer and writer on the same film, so Michael Carreras used the pen name Henry Younger for the screenplay.

An average Hammer mummy horror. It lacks a big star such as Peter Cushing. But of course it has an interesting story, setting and the usual production values that make the Hammer horror films so popular

The Curse of the Werewolf

The Curse of the Werewolf (1961)

Directed by Terence Fisher

Produced by Anthony Hinds

Written by Anthony Hinds (John Elder)

Starring:

Clifford Evans as Don Alfredo Corledo, Oliver Reed as Leon Corledo/Werewolf, Yvonne Romain as Servant girl, Catherine Feller as Christina Fernando

Leon is born in Spain on Christmas day. His mother is a mute servant girl who was raped by a beggar. She dies after his birth. Leon is a werewolf.

The film is based on the novel The Werewolf of Paris by Guy Endore. This is Oliver Reed's first credited film role.

A solid werewolf theme theme. Not too much gore or action, but it has the usual Hammer atmosphere, music and direction. The character of Leon/werewolf is very interesting too. A great performance from Oliver Reed.

Peter Cushing

Peter Cushing (1913-1994) was a British actor.

He appears in 18 Hammer horror films:

The Curse of Frankenstein (1957),
The Abominable Snowman (1957),
Dracula (1958),
The Revenge of Frankenstein (1958),
The Hound of the Baskervilles (1959),
The Mummy (1959),
The Brides of Dracula (1960),
The Evil of Frankenstein (1964),
The Gorgon (1964),
Frankenstein Created Woman (1967),
Frankenstein Must Be Destroyed (1969),
The Vampire Lovers (1970),
Twins of Evil (1971),
Dracula A.D. 1972 (1972),
Fear in the Night (1972),
The Satanic Rites of Dracula (1973),
Frankenstein and the Monster from Hell (1974),

The Legend of the 7 Golden Vampires (1974).

Cushing is one of the iconic names in Hammer horror. He plays Van Helsing in his Hammer Dracula films, and Baron von Frankenstein in his Hammer Frankenstein films. Other roles include Sherlock Holmes in The Hound of the Baskervilles, archaeologist John Banning in the Mummy, Dr. Namaroff in The Gorgon, as Dr John Rollason in The Abominable Snowman.

Cushing was born in Kenley in Surrey. He worked as a surveyor, then studied at the Guildhall School of Music and Drama. Between 1939 and 1941 he lived in Hollywood appearing in several films - including the Laurel and Hardy film A Chump at Oxford (1940). He then served in WW2 with the Entertainments National Service association (ENSA).

After WW2 he worked in film and on television. A famous role was as Winston Smith in Nineteen Eighty-Four for BBC television in 1954.

As well as Hammer horror films Cushing appears in films from other Horror companies such as Amicus and Tigon. These include the Amicus horror anthology films Dr. Terror's House of Horrors (1965), Torture Garden (1965), The House That Dripped Blood (1971), Tales from the Crypt (1972), Asylum (1972) and From Beyond the Grave (1974).

He played Doctor Who in two films: Dr. Who and the Daleks (1965) and Daleks – Invasion Earth: 2150 A.D. (1966).

A famous role for Cushing is Grand Moff Tarkin in Star Wars (1977). In Rogue One: A Star Wars Story (2016) Cushing's character was used in a CGI recreation.

Cushing retired to Whitstable in Kent and died of cancer in 1994.

D

Demons of the Mind

Demons of the Mind (1972)

Directed by Peter Sykes

Produced by Michael Carreras and Frank Godwin

Written by Christopher Wicking

Starring:

Robert Hardy as Zorn, Shane Briant as Emil, Gillian Hills as Elizabeth, Yvonne Mitchell as Hilda

A man in Bavaria locks up his two children, scared they will go mad like his wife. He gets a doctor with strange methods to supervise their health, but murders start occurring in the house.

Marianne Faithfull was going to play the role of Elizabeth, and Dirk Bogarde turned down a role in the film.

This is a thoughtful psychological horror with a good Gothic Bavarian setting. The film, a seventies Hammer, is more violent than other films by the studio. Patrick Magee is wonderful as usual as the strange doctor.

The Devil Rides Out

The Devil Rides Out (1968)

Directed by Terence Fisher

Produced by Anthony Nelson Keys

Written by Richard Matheson (based on the novel The Devil Rides Out by Dennis Wheatley).

Starring:

Christopher Lee as Nicholas, Duc de Richleau, Charles Gray as Mocata, Niké Arrighi as Tanith Carlisle, Leon Greene as Rex Van Ryn

Nicholas meets an old friend Rex. They visit Simon (Patrick Mower), the son of an old friend. Simon is meeting twelve friends at his house and black magic expert Nicholas suspects Simon is indulging in occult practices. He then learns he is part of a satanic cult run by Mocata.

The film is adapted from Denis Wheatley's novel The Devil Rides Out. Known as The Devil's Bride in the US. Lee suggested that Hammer buy the film rights to Wheatley's novel. It was not a big success at the box office, and further planned adventures featuring Lee's Duc de Richleau character were scrapped. Christopher Lee said this was one of his favourite films he appeared in.

A great satanic themed thriller - one of Hammer's best horrors. Christopher Lee is wonderful - as a hero this time. Charles Grey is great as the villain. It's very stylish. Richard Mathieson provides the screenplay and the film looks wonderful.

Dracula A.D. 1972

Dracula A.D. 1972 (1972)

Directed by Alan Gibson

Produced by Michael Carraras and Jospehine Douglas

Written by Don Houghton

Starring:

Christopher Lee as Count Dracula, Peter Cushing as Van Helsing, Stephanie Beacham as Jessica Van Helsing, Christopher Neame as Johnny Alucard

In the prologue, Van Helsing and Dracula battle in 1872 and both are killed. A follower of Dracula (played by Neame) buries Dracula's remains in St. Bartolph's Church. A hundred years later in 1972 Johnny Alucard - who looks like the man who buried Dracula's remains in 1872, invite his young friends to a black magic ceremony at the now deconsecrated St. Bartolphs's Church. In the ceremony Dracula is resurrected.

This is the seventh film in Hammer's Dracula series. It is the first with a contemporary setting. This was to try and freshen up the series and gain new fans. Count Yorga, Vampire (1970) was a successful contemporary horror, so Warner commissioned two modern set vampires films from Hammer - the first of which was Dracula A.D. 1972. The film sees the first appearance of Peter Cushing as Van Helsing since The Brides of Dracula (1968), and is the first to star Cushing and Lee since Dracula (1958).

Dracula A.D. 1972 is considered by many to be a weak Hammer film. But it has so much going for it. It has great cast with Lee and Cushing together again, and an appearance by cult British film actress Caroline Munro. The 70s London setting is very appealing to modern audiences. Great fun and a cult film.

Dracula: Prince of Darkness

Dracula: Prince of Darkness (1966)

Directed by Terence fisher

Produced by Anthony Nelson Keys

Written by Jimmy Sangster and Anthony Hinds

Starring:

Christopher Lee as Count Dracula, Narbara Shelley as Helen Kent, Andrew Keir as Father Sandor, Francis Matthews as Charles Kent

Four English tourists - the Kents - are advised not to visit
Karlsbad. They do so, and when their coach driver
abandons them because he is scared, the coach takes them
to the Count Dracula's castle. Klove, the servant of the late
Count Dracula, gives them a warm welcome.

This is a sequel to the original Dracula (1958), set 10 years
later. Christopher Lee does not have any dialogue in the
film as - according to him - he did not think Dracula's
lines were any good!

This third entry in the Hammer Dracula series is a classic
with the return of Christopher Lee in his iconic Count
Dracula role. Andrew Keir is wonderful in Van Helsing
type role as an Abbot, and the film stars Hammer beauties
Susan Farmer and Barbara Shelley. One of the classic
Hammer horror films.

Dracula Has Risen from the Grave

Dracula Has Risen from the Grave (1968)

Directed by Freddie Francis

Produced by Aida Young

Written by Anthony Hinds

Starring:

Christopher Lee as Count Dracula, Rupert Davies as
Monsignor Ernest Muller, Vernonica Carlson as Maria
Muller, Barry Andrews as Paul Paxton

In 1905 a young alter boy in a village in eastern Europe discovers the corpse of a woman in a church tower. A year later Monsignor Muller finds that the boy is now a fearful mute and everyone in the village has lost their faith. Muller exorcises the castle with the help of the local priest., But the priest has an accident which gives him a head wound which inadvertently revives the Count. The Count takes control of the priest and wants revenge on Muller.

This is the fourth entry in Hammer's Dracula series.

Another quintessential Hammer Gothic horror which is stylishly shot with great sets and score. It has a great cast with the usual selection of colourful characters and attractive women such as Veronica Carlson. It's campness adds to its cult value. It may be a bit slow paced, and maybe Dracula does not appear enough, but it another classic entry in the Hammer Dracula series.

Dracula Series

Hammer made a number of films about the Dracula legend.

In total, nine were made.

Dracula (1958),
The Brides of Dracula (1960),
Dracula: Prince of Darkness (1966),
Dracula Has Risen from the Grave (1968),
Taste the Blood of Dracula (1970),
Scars of Dracula (1970), Dracula A.D. 1972 (1972),
The Satanic Rites of Dracula (1973),

The Legend of the 7 Golden Vampires (1974)

Hammer had made a very successful film of Frankenstein
with The Curse of Frankenstein (1957), and were keen to
use another famous horror character to see if the success
could be repeated. They decided to make a Dracula film.
Hammer had difficulty financing the film, and there were
some creative arguments., but Dracula was a box office hit
in 1958 breaking records in the UK and US.

The next five films in the series - The Brides of Dracula
(1960), Dracula: Prince of Darkness (1966), Dracula Has
Risen from the Grave (1968),Taste the Blood of Dracula
(1970), Scars of Dracula (1970) - were sequels to the
original.

Hammer then made two 1970s set films - Dracula A.D.
1972 (1972), and The Satanic Rites of Dracula (1973), and
ended with the Hong Kong martial arts film The Legend of
the 7 Golden Vampires (1974).

Dr. Jekyll and Sister Hyde

Dr. Jekyll and Sister Hyde (1971)

Directed by Roy Ward Baker

Produced by Brian Clemens and Albert Fennell

Written by Brian Clemens

Starring:

Ralph Bates as Dr. Henry Jekyll/Jack the Ripper, Martine Beswick as Sister Hyde, Gerald Sim as Professor Robertson, Lewis Fiander as Howard Spencer

Dr. Henry Jekyll tries to create a potion which will extend life made from female hormones from recently dead people. Dr. Jekyll drinks the potion - and transforms into a woman - Mrs Hyde. Dr. Jekyll then has to kill young kills to get more hormones for his potion.

This is Hammer's third film based on Robert Louis Stevenson's novel Strange Case of Dr Jekyll and Mr Hyde. The others are The Ugly Duckling (1959), which is a comedy and The Two Faces of Dr. Jekyll (1960). Caroline Munro was going to play Sister Hyde, but turned the part down as it required nude scenes.

A fun new twist on the Jekyll and Hyde story. This also has the Jack the Ripper and Burke and Hare legends thrown in too! This is an entertaining seventies Hammer with some nudity and gore. Good performances from Ralph Bates and Martine Beswick.

E

Elstree Studios

Elstree Studios is the name for a number of studios that have been based around the area od Borehamwood and Elstree in Hertfordshire. Films have been made in the area since 1914. Many films and television shows have been made at the studio such as the original Star Wars trilogy and the Indiana Jones films.

After Hammer left Bray Studios in 1967, they made many of their films at Elstree.

The Evil of Frankenstein

The Evil of Frankenstein (1964)

Directed by Freddie Francis

Produced by Anthony Hinds

Written by John Elder

Starring:

Peter Cushing as Baron Victor Frankenstein, Peter Woodthorpe as Zoltan, Duncan Lamont as Chief of Police, Sandor Eles as Hans

Frankenstein continues his experiments as his family castle near Karlstaad. With the help of Zoltan, a mesmerist, he re-animates a creature he was previously working on.

This is the third in the Hammer Frankenstein series, made six years after the previous entry The Revenge of Frankenstein (1958). Hammer had a distribution deal with Universal Pictures which meant that the creature and sets could resemble those of Universal's classic Frankenstein films. Freddie Francis directed because Terence Fisher was unavailable due to a car accident.

This entry in the series discard the continuity of the first two films with a less evil Baron Frankenstein. It's a more simple film and a homage to the Universal Frankenstein. Cushing and the production values are up to the usual great standards.

F

Fear in the Night

Fear in the Night (1972)

Directed by Jimmy Sangster

Produced by Jimmy Sangster

Written by Jimmy Sangster and Michael Syson

Starring:

Judy Geeson as Peggy Heller, Joan Collins as Molly Carmichael, Peter Cushing as Michael Carmichael, Ralph Bates as Robert Heller

A woman (Peggy Heller) is recovering from a nervous breakdown. She moves with her husband to a school for boys. She is attacked by a strange man with one arm, but no one believes her story.

Another suspense-thriller-horror from Hammer. This is a solid entry in the genre which is elevated by a great cast - including presence of Joan Collins and Peter Cushing who play husband and wife!

First Hammer Horror Film

The first Hammer Horror film was The Mystery of the Mary Celeste (1935). This was released in the US as Phantom Ship.

Terence Fisher

Terence Fisher (1904-1980) was a British film director.

He directed 17 Hammer horror films:

The Curse of Frankenstein (1957),

Dracula (1958),

The Revenge of Frankenstein (1958),

The Hound of the Baskervilles (1959),

The Mummy (1959),

The Man Who Could Cheat Death (1959),

The Stranglers of Bombay (1959),

The Two Faces of Dr. Jekyll (1960),

The Curse of the Werewolf (1960),

The Brides of Dracula (1960),

The Phantom of the Opera (1962),

The Gorgon (1964),

Dracula: Prince of Darkness (1966),

Frankenstein Created Woman (1967),

The Devil Rides Out (1968),

Frankenstein Must Be Destroyed (1969),

Frankenstein and the Monster from Hell (1973)

Terence fisher was born in London in 1904.

He worked as an editor at the start of his career in the film industry. His films directed for Gainsborough such as Astonished Heart (1949) and So Long at the Fair (1950) showed him to be a talented director. In 1948 he directed his first film A Song for Tomorrow. In 1951 he directed his first film for Hammer, a thriller called The Last Page.

In 1957 Hammer invited him to direct their first colour horror film The Curse of Frankenstein. The film was a hit and Fisher went on to direct numerous other horror films.

Although at the time his horror films were not critically acclaimed, Fisher's directing is very well respected today. As a British Film Institute article said "his measured and stately style was a key aspect of the Hammer formula."

He died in 1980, aged 76.

Freddie Francis

Freddie Francis (1917-2007) was a British director and cinematographer.

He directed three Hammer horror films: The Evil of Frankenstein (1963), Nightmare (1964) and Dracula Has Risen from the Grave (1968).

Francis was born in London. Aged 16 he started work as a stills photographer, and then gained work in the film industry as a camera loader, focus puller and clapper boy. During WW2 Francis worked as a cameraman and director for army training films. After the war he worked as a camera operator, and then a cinematographer.

He moved into directing with Two and Two Make Six (1962). Many of the films he directed were horror films - his first horror directing role was on Paranoiac (1963). As well as Hammer films, he directed films for Amicus and Tyburn. His Amicus work included Dr. Terror's House of Horrors (1965), Torture Garden (1968) and Tales From The Crypt (1972).

He moved back into cinematography in the 1980s working on films such as The Elephant Man (1980), Dune (1984), Glory (1989) and The Straight Story (1999). He was a very well regarded cinematographer and won two Oscars for Best Cinematographer for Sons and Lovers (1960) and Glory (1989)

He died in 2007 aged 89.

Frankenstein

Hammer produced films based around Mary Shelley's novel Frankenstein. In all seven films were made:

The Curse of Frankenstein (1957),

The Revenge of Frankenstein (1958),

The Evil of Frankenstein (1964),

Frankenstein Created Woman (1967),

Frankenstein Must Be Destroyed (1969),

The Horror of Frankenstein (1970),

Frankenstein and the Monster from Hell (1974)

In the late 50s a Frankenstein script was submitted to

Associated Artists Productions - an American company
which Hammer was looking to work with. The script was
written by Americans Max J. Rosenberg and Milton
Subotsky, who later founded the famous British horror
film studio Amicus. The script was revised by Jimmy
Sangster, and The Curse of Frankenstein was a box office
hit when it was released in 1957. It's Gothic setting and
increased gore inspired American filmmakers such as
Roger Corman, and the famous horror filmmakers in Italy.

Peter Cushing played the role of Baron Frankenstein in six
of the films; he did not appear in The Horror of
Frankenstein (1970).

Frankenstein and the Monster from Hell

Frankenstein and the Monster from Hell (1974)

Directed by Terence Fisher

Produced by Roy Skeggs

Written by John Elder

Starring:

Peter Cushing as Baron Victor Frankenstein, Shane Briant
as Dr Simon Helder, Madeline Smith as Sarah Klauss,
David Prowse as the Creature/Herr Schneider

Frankenstein hides in an insane asylum in order to
continue with his experiments. He is helped by Dr Helder,
an inmate who been committed to the asylum for

conducting experiments similar to Frankenstein's.

This is the seventh and last of Hammer's Frankenstein films. It was filmed in 1972, but not actually released until 1974. The film did not do well at the box office.

A final appearance of Peter Cushing's classic Victor Frankenstein character. It's a good last outing with great direction by Terence Fisher and music from James Bernard. The insane asylum setting fits the Hammer Gothic horror well.

Frankenstein Created Woman

Frankenstein Created Woman (1967)

Directed by Terence Fisher

Produced by Anthony Nelson Keys

Written by Anthony Hinds (as John Elder)

Starring:

Peter Cushing as Baron Victor Frankenstein, Susan Denberg as Christina, Thorley Walters as Dr Hertz, Robert Morris as Hans

Baron Frankenstein's dead and frozen body is re-animated by Dr Hertz. This proves to Frankenstein that the soul does not leave the body upon death. His assistant Hans is executed after being accused of murdering the local pub owner after an argument. Hans's girlfriend Christina commits suicide. Frankenstein brings Christina back to life with Hans's brain inserted in place of Christina's. Hans - now in Christina's body - sets out to get revenge on those who killed him.

This is the fourth film in Hammer's Frankenstein series.

Frankenstein Created Woman is an interesting entry in the series with lots of ideas being explored with Frankenstein's attempts to transfer souls to other bodies. As usual the production values are wonderful.

Frankenstein Must Be Destroyed

Frankenstein Must Be Destroyed (1969)

Directed by Terence fisher

Produced by Anthony Nelson Keys

Written by Bert Batt

Starring:

Peter Cushing as Baron Victor Frankenstein, Veronica Carlson as Anna Spengler, George Pravda as Dr. Frederick Brandt, Freddie Jones as Professor Richter

Frankenstein is working with a young doctor Karl and Anna, Karl's fiance. Karl is working at the local insane asylum. He is stealing narcotics from the asylum, and Frankenstein uses this to blackmail Karl and Anna into working for him. Karl helps Frankenstein kidnap Dr

Brandt, a former collaborator of Frankenstein's, who has gone insane. Frankenstein wants to operate on Brandt's brain to cure him. But Brandt suffers a heart attack, so Frankenstein transplants Brandt's brain into the asylum director Professor Richter's body.

This is the fifth in the series of Frankenstein films.

James Carreras, a Hammer executive, insisted on putting a scene in the film where Frankenstein rapes Anna. Cushing, Carlson and Fisher objected to the scene and many fans of Hammer do not like it. There is no mention of the rape afterwards and the scene was not in the original script.

Another entertaining entry in the series with Cushing in fine form as the evil, scheming Victor Frankenstein. The film is slightly more sexual and gory, showing Hammer's move to more adult films to make their productions more popular as they moved into the 70s.

G

Tudor Gates

Tudor Gates (1930-2007) was a British screenwriter and playwright .

He wrote the screenplay for three Hammer horror films: The Vampire Lovers (1970), Lust for a Vampire (1971) and Twins of Evil (1971).

Gates worked in stage management early in his career and

then moved into screenwriting. After writing for television, he wrote the screenplay for cult sixties films Danger: Diabolik (1968) and Barbarella (1968).

He wrote the Hammer Karnstein Trilogy of films in the 70s.

John Gilling

John Gilling (1912-1984) was a British director and screenwriter.

He directed four Hammer films:

The Shadow of the Cat (1961),

The Plague of the Zombies (1966),

The Reptile (1966),

The Mummy's Shroud (1967).

Gilling moved to Hollywood aged 17 to do various jobs in the film industry. In the 1930s he worked in Britain as an editor and assistant director. After serving on the Royal Navy during WW2, he worked as a screenwriter and director. Gilling worked on many low detective and thriller films, and also directed for television on programmes such as The Saint and Department S.

He wrote many screenplays - including Hammer films The Gorgon (1964), The Mummy's Shroud (1967)

He directed his first Hammer Horror film in 1961 -

Shadow of the Cat.

He died in Madrid in Spain in 1984.

The Gorgon

The Gorgon (1964)

Directed by Terence Fisher

Produced by Anthony Nelson Keys

Written by John Gilling

Starring:

Christopher Lee as Professor Karl Meister, Peter Cushing as Dr. Namaroff, Richard Pasco as Paul Heitz, Barbara Shelley as Carla Hoffman/Megaera

In a German village in 1910 a number of murders have been committed over 5 years. Each victim has been turned into stone. Local authorities are scared the murders are part of a legend, but a man investigates.

The film is based on the Greek legend of the Gorgon, a creature that turns those who look at it to stone.

A fine Hammer take on the Gorgon legend. It's very atmospheric and has the legendary team of Cushing and Lee - although they are not on screen together that much.

Val Guest

Val Guest (1911-2006) was a British director and screenwriter.

He directed The Quatermass Xperiment (1955), giving it its documentary, social realist feel. Other Hammer horror films include Quatermass 2 (1957) and The Abominable Snowman (1957).

Guest directed other non horror films for Hammer.

Early in his career he worked mainly in comedies. After The Quatermass Xperiment he worked on numerous dramas, crime and war and science fiction films. He also directed for television.

H

Hammer Presents Dracula with Christopher Lee

Hammer Presents Dracula with Christopher Lee is a music album released by EMI in 1974.

Side 1 of the LP has a new Dracula story written by Don Houghton. It is narrated by Christopher Lee and has music by James Bernard. Side 2 has music from Fear in the Night, She, The Vampire Lovers and Dr Jekyll and Sister Hyde. The music for side 2 is arranged by Philip Martell. The album was released later as a CD.

Hands of the Ripper

Hands of the Ripper (1971)

Directed by Peter Sasdy

Produced by Aida Young

Written by L.W. Davidson and Edward Spencer Shew

Starring:

Eric Porter as Dr. John Pritchard, Angharad Rees as Anna, Jane Merrow as Laura, Keith Bell as Michael Pritchard

Jack the Ripper's daughter sees her father kill her mother when she is young. When she grows up she is troubled and possessed by the spirit of her father. She kills like her father - but when in a trance. A psychiatrist tries to cure her.

Some of the film was filmed at St. Paul's Cathedral in London.

This is a rather gory and scary Hammer horror film, showing the more adult tone of seventies Hammer films. The film has some interesting psychological elements and an early 1900s setting.

Anthony Hinds

Anthony Hinds (1922-2013) was a British screenwriter and producer.

Hinds was born in London and served a pilot during WW2. He is the son of the founder of Hammer Films William Hinds, and worked extensively for the company after WW2.

Hinds had the idea of adapting the BBC television play The Quatermass Xperiment for the cinema. The film, released in 1955, was a big success and made Hammer make more horror films. Hammer Executive Michael Carreras said "The film that must take all the credit for the whole Hammer series of horror films was really The Quatermass Xperiment".

Hinds also thought of using country houses for exterior and interior shots, saving money on using a normal studio. This led to Hammer buying Down Place which became the iconic Bray Studios.

Hammer could not afford a screenwriter for 1961's The Curse of the Werewolf. Hinds penned a script using the alias John Elder and went on to write numerous screenplays for Hammer using the pseudonym. He wrote Hammer films such as The Evil of Frankenstein (1964), Dracula: Prince of Darkness (1966), The Mummy's Shroud (1967), Dracula Has Risen From the Grave (1968), Scars of Dracula (1970) and Frankenstein and the Monster From Hell (1974).

He died in 2013 aged 91.

William Hinds

William Hinds (1887–1957) was a film studio executive

Hinds was involved in owning music halls and producing shows for summer seasons and the theatre.

In 1934 he launched Hammer Productions. The company went into liquidation, but was reformed in 1946 as Hammer Film Productions. His son Anthony Hinds was a screenwriter and producer at Hammer films for many years.

The Horror of Frankenstein

The Horror of Frankenstein (1970)

Directed by Jimmy Sangster

Produced by Jimmy Sangster

Written by Jimmy Sangster and Jeremy Burnham

Starring:

Ralph Bates and Baron Victor Frankenstein, Kate O'Mara as Alys, Veronica Carlson as Elizabeth Heiss, Dennis Price as The Graverobber

Victor Frankenstein creates a man from various body parts. The monster comes alive and causes havoc.

This is the sixth in Hammer's Frankenstein series. But it is not really part of the series. Cushing is absent, and it is a separate remake of the first 1957 film, The Curse of Frankenstein.

This is not a critically acclaimed film but, as is often the case with Hammer, it is certainly a cult film. This is a different type of Frankenstein film from the Cushing series with a more erotic and gory tone typical of Hammer's early 70s horrors. It is great fun and Ralph Bates is very charismatic in his role as Victor Frankenstein.

The Hound of the Baskervilles

The Hound of the Baskervilles (1959)

Directed by Terence Fisher

Produced by Michael Carreras, Anthony Hinds, Anthony Nelson Keys and Kenneth Hyman

Screenplay by Peter Bryan (based on the novel by Arthur Conan Doyle

Starring:

Peter Cushing as Sherlock Holmes, André Morell as Doctor Watson, Christopher Lee as Sir Henry Baskerville, Marla Landi as Cecile Stapleton

Sherlock Holmes and Dr Watson investigate the death of Sir Charles Baskerville in the rural West Country of England the location of Baskerville Hall. It is believed that a mysterious hound killed Sir Charles, and that a hound also killed Sir Hugo Baskerville - an ancestor of Sir Charles - in the past. Holmes and Watson investigate meeting up with the new owner of Baskerville Hall - Sir Henry.

This is a Hammer version of the classic Sherlock Holmes tale. There a number of changes from the novel. Peter Cushing played Holmes in a well regarded BBC television series in the 1960s.

The Hound of the Baskervilles is a critically acclaimed adaption of the novel. Cushing does one of the best portrayals of Holmes on screen. Morell is great as Watson and Christopher Lee adds great presence to the film as usual. The Hammer Gothic style - sets, music etc - suits the famous story and this is one of the best Hammer horror films.

Don Houghton

Don Houghton (1930-1991) was a British scriptwriter.

He wrote the screenplays for the Hammer horror films Dracula A.D. 1972, The Satanic Rites of Dracula (1973) and The Legend of the 7 Golden Vampires (1974).

He wrote extensively for television and radio, and created the Scottish soap opera Take the High Road (1980).

K

Andrew Keir

Andrew Keir (1926-1997) was a British actor.

He appears in three Hammer horror films: Dracula: Prince of Darkness (1966), Quatermass and the Pit (1967) and Blood from the Mummy's Tomb (1971).

In Dracula: Prince of Darkness he plays Father Sandor. In Quatermass and the Pit he plays Professor Bernard Quatermass. In Blood From the Mummy's Tomb he plays Julian Fuchs.

Keir was born in Scotland and worked as a coal miner from the age of 14. He became interested in amateur dramatics and got a job as an actor at a theatre in Glasgow during WW2.

From the 1950s he had numerous film and television roles, including Cleopatra (1963), Zeppelin (1971), Daleks – Invasion Earth: 2150 A.D. (1966).

He worked extensively in the theatre.

Keir died in 1997.

The Kiss of the Vampire

The Kiss of the Vampire (1963)

Directed by Don Sharp

Produced by Anthony Hinds

Written by John Elder

Starring:

Clifford Evans as Professor Zimmer, Noel Willman as Dr. Ravna, Edward de Souza as Gerald Harcourt, Jennifer Daniel as Marianne Harcourt

Gerald and Marianne Harcourt car breaks down in Bavaria forcing them to spend a few days in a remote village. They are offered rooms as Dr Ravna's castle. Dr Ravna is the head of a vampire cult.

The film was going to be another entry - the third - in Hammer's Dracula series of films. In the end it was a stand alone vampire film without Dracula in it.

A lavish if slightly slow moving vampire film from Hammer. It has the usual wonderful production values with great music from James Bernard. No Hammer Dracula icons appear, but there are good performances from the cast.

L

Christopher Lee

Sir Christopher Lee (1922-2015) was a British actor.

He appears in 18 Hammer horror films.:

The Curse of Frankenstein (1957),

Dracula (1958),

The Hound of the Baskervilles (1959),

The Man Who Could Cheat Death (1959),

The Mummy (1959), The Two Faces of Dr. Jekyll (1960),

The Terror of the Tongs (1961),

The Gorgon (1964),

Dracula: Prince of Darkness (1966),

Rasputin, the Mad Monk (1966),

The Devil Rides Out (1968),

Dracula Has Risen from the Grave (1968),

Taste the Blood of Dracula (1970),

Scars of Dracula (1970),

Dracula A.D. 1972 (1972),

The Satanic Rites of Dracula (1973),

To the Devil a Daughter (1976),

The Resident (2011)

Christopher Lee's most iconic role was as Count Dracula. He plays the role in seven Hammer films. He also play the monster in Frankenstein (1957) along with a variety of memorable leading Hammer roles.

Lee as born in London. In WW2 he volunteered for the Finnish Army. He then trained as an RAF pilot, bur injured his eye so was unable to fly and joined RAF intelligence. Lee had many intelligence missions in Africa and Italy during the war.

After the war Lee's cousin Nicolò Carandini, who was the Italian Ambassador to Britain, suggested he become an actor. Lee joined Rank Studios and his career started with bit parts.

Lee has made many films. He made many horror films for

studios other than Hammer. His most famous include The Wicker Man (1973), a horror on which he plays the villain Lord Summerisle. The James Bond film The Man With the Golden Gun (1974) where he plays the villain Scaramanga. Lee played Fu Manchu five times in the 1960s.

A big later role for Lee was as Saruman in The Lord of the Ring's trilogy of films made between 2001-2003. In Star Wars: Episode II – Attack of the Clones (2002) and Star Wars: Episode III – Revenge of the Sith (2005) he plays Count Dooku.

Lee also had many television roles in Britain, the US and elsewhere. His varied career as a popular icon led him to do many different projects. He had an operatic bass voice and performed songs in several films. He even released a heavy metal album!

Lee died aged 93 in 2015.

The Legend of the 7 Golden Vampires

The Legend of the 7 Golden Vampires

Directed by Roy Ward Baker and Chang Cheh

Produced by Don Houghton and Wee King Shaw

Written by Don Houghton

Starring:

Peter Cushing as Professor Lawrence Van Helsing, John Forbes-Robertson as Count Dracula, Robin Stewart as Leyland Van Helsing, Julie Ege as Vanessa Buren

In 1804 a man is going into the Castle Deacula in Transyvanoia. He summons Dracula, and says he is Kah, a Taoist monk who is High Priest of the Seven Golden Vampires in China. Kah needs Dracula to revive the Golden Vampire's powers. Dracula needs Kah's body to escape the Castle, he takes it and leaves. In 1904 Van Helsing is lecturing in China. He hears of a village being attacked by a vampire cult - the Seven Golden Vampires.

This is the ninth - and final - film in the Hammer Dracula series. It was a co production of Hammer and the famous Hong Kong Shaw Brothers Studio. Christopher Lee does not appear as Dracula. The role is played by John Forbes-Robertson, who played a Dracula type character (The Man in Black) in The Vampire Lovers. Dracula is voiced by David de Keyser. Hammer were looking to cash in on the popularity of Kung Fu movies at the time with this entry.

The film is a combination of a seventies Hammer film and a seventies Hong Kong action martial arts films. It is therefore bound to be over the top, fun and entertaining.

The presence of the legendary Peter Cushing makes this a wonderful and colourful end to the Hammer Dracula series.

Lust for a Vampire

Lust for a Vampire (1971)

Directed by Jimmy Sangster

Produced by Michael Style and Harry Fine

Written by Tudor Gates (based on characters created by Sheridan Le Fanu)

Starring:

Yutte Stensgaard as Mircalla Herritzen/Carmilla Karnstein, Michael Johnson as Richard LeStrange, Ralph Bates as Giles Barton, Barbara Jefford as Countess Herritzen

Miricalla arrives at a finishing school in Styria. Author Richard Lestrange and the school's headmaster fall in love with her. Miricalla is a vampire and those who suspect start to disappear.

Lust for a Vampire is the second film in the Karnstein Trilogy. The other films in the trilogy are The Vampire Lovers (1970) and Twins of Evil (1971). The trilogy is based on the J. Sheridan Le Fanu novel Carmilla. This is more adult in tone as is the whole trilogy, with extra gore and more erotic tone with the lesbian vampire theme. Ingrid Pitt played Carmilla in the previous film in the trilogy, but turned down the chance to return here. Peter Cushing was unavailable as he was caring for his wife. Ralph Bates called the film "one of the worst films ever made"!

This is a by the numbers seventies Hammer Horror, but naturally still wonderful for fans of the genre. It's very erotic and glamorous with actresses such as the Yutte Stensgaard, Suzanna Leigh and Pippa Steel. Stensgaard is fabulous, but there is not Cushing or Lee, or a director such as Terence Fisher. Mike Raven has great cult value but he is not as iconic as Christopher Lee.

M

Philip Martell

Philip Martell (1907-1993) was a British composer and musical director.

He was the head of Hammer Studio's music department.

Martell went to the Guildhall School of Music. Early in his career he conducted musicals, and started arranging film music in the 1930s. In 1954 he joined Hammer, and in 1963 became the musical director. He worked on numerous Hammer horror films as musical director. He composers for many Hammer horror films and oversaw their scores.

Aside from Hammer he worked as a musical director on various film and television productions.

Mummy

Hammer made four films based on the Mummy character. Four films were made: The Mummy (1959), The Curse of Mummy's Tomb (1964), The Mummy's Shroud (1967) and Blood From the Mummy's Tomb (1971).

The films used Universal's Mummy character which they introduced in The Mummy (1932). Hammer made a deal with Universal to make horror films using Universal monster characters such as the Mummy, Frankenstein and Dracula.

The Mummy

The Mummy (1959)

Directed by Terence Fisher

Produced by Michael Carreras and Anthony Nelson Keys

Written by Jimmy Sangster

Starring:

Peter Cushing as John Banning, Christopher Lee as Kharis, Yvonne Furneaux as Isobel Banning/Princess Ananka, Eddie Byrne as Inspector Mulrooney

In the late 19th Century, a team of British archaeologists in Egypt discover the tomb of Princess Ananka, and bring the mummified body of her High Priest to life. In England three years later a follower of the Princess brings uses the mummy to gain revenge on the archaeologists.

This first Hammer Mummy film uses plot and characters from the Universal Mummy films Mummy's Hand (1940) and The Mummy's Tomb (1940). 1958's Hammer Dracula film was a success, so Universal gave Hammer the remake rights to their monster movies. The Mummy was a big success breaking box office records in the US and UK.

An early Hammer classic and the first in their Mummy series. This has the usual wonderful production values and the presence of Peter Cushing and Christopher Lee. This atmospheric colourful film helped create the classic look of the Hammer horror films.

The Mummy's Shroud

The Mummy's Shroud (1967)

Directed by John Gilling

Produced by Michael Carreras

Written by John Gilling and Anthony Hinds

Starring:

Andre Morell as Sir Basil Walden, John Phillips as Stanley Preston, David Buck as Paul Preston, Elizabeth Sellars as Barbara Preston

A team of British archaeologists in 1920 find the tomb of the boy Pharaoh Kah-To-Bey. They soon find themselves being killed by the Mummy...

This is the third film in the Hammer Mummy series. It was the last Hammer film to be shot at Bray Studios.

This is a not a classic Hammer film. But it has all the Hammer horror elements so is very entertaining for fans of the genre. although cheaply it has a charming look, and the cast with actors Andre Morell and Michael Ripper is good.

Caroline Munro

Caroline Munro (1949-) is a British actress.

She appears in: Dracula A.D. 1972 (1972) and Captain Kronos - Vampire Hunter (1974).

In Dracula A.D. 1972 she plays Laura. In Captain Kronos - Vampire Lover, Munro has a big role as the lover of the hero Kronos.

Her other film roles include a the comedy western Talent for Loving (1969), as Dr Phibes's wife Victoria Regina in The Abominable Dr Phibes (1971) and Dr. Phibes Rises Again (1972)., as Margiana in The Golden Voyage of Sinbad (1973), At The Earth's Core (1979) the science fiction film where she played Dia, as the villain Naomi in James Bond film The Spy Who Loved Me (1977), the US slasher horror Maniac (1980) where Munro has a big role as Anna, the Italian Star Wars influenced Starcrash (1979) where she plays Stella Star, and Demons 6: De Profundis (1989) where she played Nora.

Her television roles include appearing as hostess on the popular British game show 3-2-1 between 1984-87, in the Frankie Howerd series The Howard Confessions and The New Avengers.

She turned down a few Hammer roles as they required her to be nude in scenes. These films were Dr Jekyll and Sister Hyde and Frankenstein and the Monster From Hell.

The Mystery of the Mary Celeste

The Mystery of the Mary Celeste (1935)

Directed by Denison Clift

Produced by Henry Passmore

Written by Denison Clift and Charles Larkworthy

Starring:

Bela Lugosi as Anton Lorenzen, Shirley Grey as Sarah Briggs, Arthur Margetson as Capt. Benjamin Briggs

The crew on a ship realise there is a murderer amongst them.

The story is based on the case of the Mary Celeste, the sailing ship which was found deserted in the Atlantic Ocean in 1872. This film depicts a fictional scenario of what might have happened.

The US version is the only version that now exists. It is 18 minutes shorter than the original version.

The film is an atmospheric vintage chiller with a cast that includes the legendary horror actor Bela Lugosi.

N

Nightmare

Nightmare (1964)

Directed by Freddie Francis

Produced by Jimmy Sangster

Written by Jimmy Sangster

Starring:

David Knight as Henry Baxter, Moira Redmond as Grace Maddox, Jennie Linden as Janet, Brenda Bruce as Mary Lewis

Janet is a student at a private school. She has nightmares where her mother (who is in an asylum) haunting her. she is sent home from the school, and her nightmares continue.

Jennie Linden was a late replacement for Julie Christie.

This is a good thriller. The atmosphere is helped by the black and white film and the direction by Freddie Francis.

O

Oakley Court

Oakley Court is a Gothic house built in 1859. It is located in Berkshire on the river Thames.

Hammer studios used the house as an office in 1949. They used the building as a location for several films. Exterior scenes for The Brides of Dracula (1962), The Reptile (1966), and The Plague of the Zombies (1966) were filmed at Oakley.

Many other films used the location such as The Rocky Horror Picture Show (1975).

Oakley Court

P

Ingrid Pitt

Ingrid Pitt (1037-2010) was a Polish-British actress.

She appears in: The Vampire Lovers (1970) and Countess Dracula (1971).

In The Vampire Lovers she plays Marcilla/Carmilla/Mircalla Karnstein in a more erotic Hammer entry. In Countess Dracula Pitt plays Countess Elisabeth Nadasdy, a countess in 17th Century Hungary who bathes in the blood of youthful women to keep her youth.

Other film appearances by Pitt include Where Eagles Dare (1968), the Amucus compendium horror The House That Dripped Blood (1971), The Wicker Man (1971) and Who Dares Wins (1982).

Pitt also had numerous roles in television in such shows as Ironside and Doctor Who.

She was also a prolific writer writing numerous works of fiction as well as non fiction books on the horror genre and various articles.

Pitt was born Ingoushka Petrov in Warsaw in Poland. Her father was German-Russian, and her mother was a Jewish Pole. Her family was placed in a concentration camp during WW2. After the war she married an American and moved to the US. She then moved to Britain.

She died aged 73 in 2010.

The Phantom of the Opera

The Phantom of the Opera (1962)

Directed by Terence Fisher

Produced by Anthony Hinds and Basil Keys

Written by John Elder (based on The Phantom of the Opera by Gaston Leroux)

Starring:

Herbert Lom as The Phantom of the Opera/Professor Petrie, Heather Sears as Christine Charles, Edward de Souza as Harry Hunter, Michael Gough as Lord Ambrose D'Arcy

Lord d'Arcy steals the work of composer Professor Petrie. Petries tries to stop the printing of his stolen music but starts a fire at the printers and is disfigured. Years later Petrie returns to haunt an opera house staging one of his stolen works.

This is based on the famous story by Gaston Leroux. Universal Studios wanted to make another version of A Phantom of the Opera and let Hammer make it. The film had quite a high budget by Hammer standards.

A typically atmospheric Hammer version of a famous story. It is not really an out and out horror, but does have an eerie atmosphere. Lom and Gough are magnificent.

Pinewood Studios

Pinewood Studios is a film and television studio near Windsor in Berkshire. The studio was created in 1935 by J. Arthur Rank.

The studio has been used by many famous productions such as the James Bond series, the Christopher Reeve Superman series, the Carry On films, Marvel Studios films and the 2010s Star Wars films.

Several Hammer films were filmed at Pinewood from 1968 after Hammer moved from Bray studios.

The Plague of the Zombies

The Plague of the Zombies (1966)

Directed by John Gilling

Produced by Anthony Nelson Keys

Written by Peter Bryan

Starring:

André Morell as Sir James Forbes, Diane Clare as Sylvia Forbes, Brook Williams as Dr. Peter Tompson, Jacqueline Pearce as Alice Mary Tompson

In a village in Cornwall in 1860, the villagers are dying of a mysterious plague. Dr Tompson calls in help in the form of Sir James Forbes. Sir James uncovers a mystery involving voodoo and zombies.

This zombie film from Hammer influenced the look of zombie films that were made after it. It was shot back to back with The Reptile using the same sets made by Bernard Robinson.

Great Hammer zombie film. The sets are wonderful and the voodoo/black magic theme is very atmospheric. The end in the tin mine is very memorable, and John Carson puts in a good turn as the villain Squire Clive Hamilton.

Q

Quatermass 2

Quatermass 2 (1957)

Directed by Val Guest

Produced by Anthony Hinds

Screenplay by Nigel Kneale and Val Guest

Starring:

Brian Donlevy as Professor Bernard Quatermass, John Longden as Lomax, Sidney James as Jimmy Hall, Bryan Forbes as Marsh

Professor Quatermass sees strange meteorites on his radar.
They have been crashing down in an area of England -
Winnerden Flats. He investigates and discovers an
industrial complex which is used by aliens to infiltrate and
influence the British government. Quatermass tries to stop
them.

Quatermass 2 is a sequel to Hammer's The Quatermass
Xperiment (1955). It is based on the BBC television series
Quatermass II which was written by Nigel Kneale.

This is a solid well regarded sci fi horror. The black and
white film and locations give it a great atmosphere. The
plot about a conspiracy by aliens to take over society and a
cover up of a top secret facility by a government has been
used many times since.

Quatermass and the Pit

Quatermass and the Pit (1967)

Directed by Roy Ward Baker

Produced by Anthony Nelson Keys

Written by Nigel Kneale

Starring:

James Donald as Doctor Roney, Andrew Keir as Professor
Bernard Quatermass, Barbara Shelley as Barbara Judd,
Julian Glover as (Lieutenant) Colonel Breen

Workers at Hobbs End London Underground station did up skeletons. Paleontologist Dr Roney is called in and says they are the remains of five million year old apemen. Also discovered at the site is a metallic object. It is thought to be an unexploded bomb, so a bomb squad is brought in. Colonel Breen is brought in, accompanied by Professor Quatermass. Quatermass says the object is extraterrestrial and extraterrestrial bodies are found in it, and Quatermass suspects it has been influencing humanity.

This is the third and last film in Hammer's Quatermass series. It was made 10 years after the previous one - Quatermass 2 (1957). It is based on the BBC television series Quatermass and the Pit. Brian Donlevy who had played Quatermass in the first two film was replaced as by Andrew Keir.

Another thought provoking Hammer Quatermass film exploring issues such as the nature of evil. This one is the only Hammer Quatermass in colour which enhances the great sets. Roy Ward Baker does a good job with the direction. Another Hammer classic.

The Quatermass Xperiment

The Quatermass Xperiment (1955)

Directed by Val Guest

Produced by Anthony Hinds

Screenplay by Richard Landau and Val Guest (based on The Quatermass Experiment television play by Nigel

Kneale)

Starring:

Brian Donlevy as Prof. Bernard Quatermass, Richard Wordsworth as Victor Carroon, Jack Warner as Inspector Lomax, David King-Wood as Dr. Gordon Briscoe

A spacecraft with a crew of three returns to Earth with only one crew member (Victor Carron) who subsequently mutates into an alien organism which threatens to spawn and take over Earth. The creature escapes and Inspector Lomax must track it down.

The film is based on a BBC television serial which was made up of six episodes. Hammer bought the rights to make a film version. Richard Landau, an American, wrote the first draft of the script emphasising the horror elements of the tv series. The film was an X certificate when released in the UK, meaning that no one under 16 could watch it. Hammer was struggling to produce successful films when they made The Quatermass Xperiment. But this film was a big hit and allowed the studio to do deals with major film distributors. It also led to Hammer's move into horror and the numerous successful Hammer films in the genre.

This is a famous Hammer film as it was groundbreaking at the time of release with its levels of horror. It is a great sci f-/horror film with an extremely atmospheric film noir feel.. The story of an alien coming back to Earth in a human spacecraft has been used many times since.

R

Rasputin the Mad Monk

Rasputin the Mad Monk (1966)

Directed by Don Sharp

Produced by Anthony Nelson Keys

Written by Anthony Hinds

Starring:

Christopher Lee as Grigori Rasputin, Barbara Shelley as Sonia, Richard Pasco as Dr. Boris Zargo, Francis Matthews as Ivan

This is about Rasputin, then mysterious mystic who was an advisor to the Russian royal family before the Russian Revolution in 1917.

The film is a fictional account of Rasputin's life, with some of the story based in Prince Yusipov's account.

A good account of the strange life of Rasputin, although it is perhaps a bit cheaply made. The film shows Rasputin's magic powers. As usual Christopher Lee turns in a charismatic performance as Rasputin.

The Reptile

The Reptile (1966)

Directed by John Gilling

Produced by Anthony Nelson Keys

Written by Anthony Hinds (aka John Elder)

Starring:

Noel Willman as Dr. Franklyn, Ray Barrett as Harry George Spalding, Jennifer Daniel as Valerie Spalding, Jacqueline Pearce as Anna Franklyn

In the early 1900s locals in a Cornish village are dying from a plague. Harry Spalding inherits a house in the village and moves there with his wife Valeries. The locals are suspicious of them, but they decide to stay and investigate the cause of the deaths.

This was filmed back to back with The Plague of the Zombies, using the same sets.

This is a very good suspenseful, moody sixties horror with a great monster. Noel Willman puts in a good performance as the sinister Dr. Franklyn.

Revival

Hammer films went stopped making films in the 1970s; the last Hammer production was The Lady Vanishes

(1979). The studio went into receivership. Hammer then moved to television with two series developed by Roy Skeggs - Hammer House of Horror in 1980 and Hammer House of Mystery and Suspense in 1984. After 1984 the studio went into hiatus. a number of people tried to revive Hammer. In 2007 a new consortium bought Hammer and made several new Hammer films.

These are

Beyond the Rave (2008)

This is a very low budget vampire film set in Britain's rave scene.

Let Me In (2010)

Let Me In is an English language version of the critically acclaimed Swedish vampire film Let the Right One In (2008). Let Me In moves the story to New Mexico. It stars Kodi Smit-McPhee and Chloë Grace Moretz. Let Me In received good reviews.

The Resident (2011)

The Resident is a New York set film about a woman doctor who moves into a bargain apartment and finds the landlord has an obsession with her. It stars Hilary Swank and Jeffrey Dean Morgan. This is more of a thriller than a horror, but it does feature a cameo by Hammer horror veteran Christopher Lee.

Wake Wood (2011)

Wake wood is a horror about a couple whose young daughter has died. They move to a village called Wakewood in Northern Ireland. They find out that there is a pagan ritual in the village where people can be brought back for three days, and the couple resurrect their daughter. It had a limited release in cinemas in the UK.

The Woman in Black (2012)

This is an adaption of Susan Hil"s novel. A young solicitor - played by Daniel Rafcliffe, goes to a remote village and finds that a ghost of a woman is haunting the people. This was quite a big box office hit.

The Quiet Ones (2014)

The Quiet Ones is a low budget film 70s British set film about an experiment in to prove poltergeists are made up of the human psyche and not supernatural.

The Woman in Black: Angel of Death (2015)

This is a sequel to the Woman in Black (2012). It is set 40 years after the first film, during WW2.

The Lodge (2019)

A woman is snowed in with her fiance's two children in a holiday lodge in Massachusetts. Strange supernatural events inspired by her religious upbringing surface.

The Revenge of Frankenstein

The Revenge of Frankenstein (1958)

Directed by Terence Fisher

Produced by Anthony Hinds

Written by Jimmy Sangster

Starring:

Peter Cushing as Baron Vn Frankenstein, Francis Matthews as Dr. Hans Kleve, Eunice Gayson as Margaret, Oscar Quitk as Karl

Victor Frankenstein escapes execution by arranging a priest to be beheaded in his place. He then takes up the name of Dr Stein and becomes a physician in Carlsbruck. Dr Kleve recognises Frankenstein and blackmails him into employing Kleve as his apprentice. They continue Frankenstein's experiments to transplant a living brain into a new body.

This is a sequel to 1957's The Curse of Frankenstein.

Another classic atmospheric Hammer Gothic horror and a great entry in the Frankenstein series. This one further develops Cushing's fascinating Baron Frankenstein character.

Michael Ripper

Michael Ripper (1913-2000) was a British actor.

He appears in 16 Hammer horror films:

X the Unknown (1956),
Quatermass 2 (1957),
The Revenge of Frankenstein (1958),
The Man Who Could Cheat Death (1959),
The Mummy (1959),
The Brides of Dracula (1960),
The Curse of the Werewolf (1961),
The Phantom of the Opera (1962),
The Curse of the Mummy's Tomb (1964),
The Plague of the Zombies (1966),
Rasputin the Mad Monk (1966),
The Reptile (1966),
The Deadly Bees (1966),
Dracula Has Risen from the Grave (1968),
Taste the Blood of Dracula (1970),
Scars of Dracula (1970).

He appears in more Hammer horror films than any other
actor, many in minor roles (he is quoted as playing
"supporting character roles: coachmen, peasants, tavern
keepers..."), or even, as in Rapsutin and the Mad Monk in
a voice role only. Larger roles are in The Scars of Dracula
where he plays the pub landlord in the village, and The
Plague of the Zombies where he plays a policeman.

He was born in Portsmouth. Riper did lots of work on
stage early in his career. But in 1952 an operation as
affected his voice so he was not able to work - it reduced

the power of his voice.

Ripper appears in many films in character bit parts - lots of his early work in the 30s and 40s is uncredited. He made numerous non-horror Hammer films too, and appears in 35 Hammer films. He was friends with Hammer producer Anthony Hinds which helped him get the Hammer roles.

He had many television parts, including a famous role as Thomas th butler in the BBC sitcom Butterflies.

Bernard Robinson

Bernard Robinson (1912-1970) was a production designer. He designed the sets for many of the Hammer horror films. His crypts, castles and laboratories helped create the distinctive Hammer look. Robinson created elaborate sets, such as the Castle Dracula used in Dracula (1958). His skill was in creating great sets on a low budget. The sets he created were often used on different Hammer films.

He was born in Liverpool and worked for Warner Brothers in London early in his career.

Harry Robertson

Harry Robertson (1932-1996) was a British musician.

Robertson was born in Scotland. He studied archaeology, but became a music teacher in London. He then worked as a musical director at Decca Records and on television pop programmes such as Six-Five Special and Oh Boy! He worked in stage musical arranging and conducting the music.

He was known as Harry Robinson during some of career as he was given a cheque in the name by mistake so opened a bank account in that name!

In 1968 he wrote the theme to Journey Into the Unknown, the Hammer television series. This led to work scoring several films for Hammer such as The Vampire Lovers (1970), Countess Dracula (1971), Lust for a Vampire (1971) and Twins of Evil (1972).

For his work on Twins of Evil Robertson said:

"I had always wanted to score a western and had never been asked, so when I saw the first rushes of TWINS OF EVIL I thought, well there's horses in it and people dashing around the countryside so why not. I will do a western theme of sorts to match this. Surprisingly it worked and everyone loved it."

S

Jimmy Sangster

Jimmy Sangster (1927-2011) was a British screenwriter and director.

He directed three Hammer horror films: The Horror of Frankenstein (1970), Lust for a Vampire (1971) and Fear in the Night (1972).

He wrote numerous screenplays for Hammer horror films:

X: The Unknown (1956),
The Curse of Frankenstein (1957),
Dracula (1958),
The Revenge of Frankenstein (1958),
The Mummy (1959), The Brides of Dracula (1960),
Dracula: Prince of Darkness (1966),
The Horror of Frankenstein (1970).

Sangster worked in a number of roles for Hammer early in his career. These included roles as a second unit director, assistant director, production manager and production assistant. He then turned to scriptwriting, penning various Hammer horror films and other films such as Jack the Ripper (1959), The Pirates of Blood River (1962) and The Nanny (1965). Sangster also wrote scripts for television shows such as Wonder Woman, Cannon, Ironside and Banacek.

He died in 2011 aged 83.

Peter Sasdy

Peter Sasdy is a British film director.

He directed three Hammer horror film: Taste the Blood of Dracula (1970) Hands of the Ripper (1971) and Countess Dracula (1971).

Sasdy was born in Hungary and moved to Britain in 1956

He has directed numerous television shows on series such as Minder, Hammer House of Horror, The Return of the Saint, The Stone tape and Armchair Theatre.

Bran Castle

The Satanic Rights of Dracula

The Satanic Rights of Dracula (1973)

Directed by Alan Gibson

Produced by Roy Skeggs, Don Houghton

Written by Don Houghton

Starring:

Christopher Lee as Count Dracula, Peter Cushing as
Lorrimer Van Helsing, Michael Coles as Inspector Murray,
Willian Franklyn as Peter Torrence

In 1974, an intelligence agent escapes from a country
house in England where satanic rituals are being carried
out. He reveals four leading members of society are
involved to his superiors before dying of his wounds.
Inspector Murray is called in to work on the case, and he
employs the help of occult expert Van Helsing after
vampirism is suspected.

This is the eighth film in Hammer's Dracula series. It
reunited Lee and Cushing for the third and final time in the
Dracula series, and in Hammer horror films. The film has
much of the cast and characters of the previous Dracula,
Dracula A.D. 1972. Joanna Lumley replaces Stephanie
Beacham as Jessica Van Helsing.

The Satanic Rights of Dracula is an entertaining horror
which introduces elements of science fiction and spy
thriller. Peter Cushing is wonderful as always as Van
Helsing, and Christopher Lee has more dialogue than usual
which is welcome. It has an entertaining plot too and a
slightly offbeat atmosphere.

Scars of Dracula

Scars of Dracula (1970)

Directed by Roy Ward Baker

Produced by Aida Young

Written by Anthony Hinds

Starring:

Christopher Lee as Count Dracula, Dennis Waterman as Simon Carlson, Jenny Hanley as Sarah Framsen, Christopher Matthews as Paul Carlson

In the prologue, Dracula's remains are in a room in his castle, only accessible by a window. A bat spits blood on the remains, and the Count is resurrected. Later, local villagers are angry that the Count is killing young women again. They set fire to the Count's castle; in response the Count kills all the women and children in the village. Paul Carlson is on the run after being falsely accused of rape. He ends up at Dracula's castle. Pau's brother Simon arrives in the local village with Paul's fiancee Sarah to try and find Paul.

Scars of Dracula is the fifth Hammer Dracula entry and the second of 1970. It is the last of the period Dracula films: subsequent entries would be set in the present day.

Many Hammer fans do the like this because of the weaker cast and cheaper sets. But it is an entertaining entry in the series with all the trademark elements of the Dracula series. The increased role for Christopher Lee helps too.

Sex

Hammer films were famous for their sexual content, particularly in the 1970s films. Hammer horror films of the 60s and 60s were quite erotic dealing with sexual themes and with glamorous women in rather risque outfits often showing lots of cleavage.

From the late 1960s horror films in Europe and the US became more explicit with sex and nudity. Hammer tried to keep up with these market changes and their 70s films had more nudity and more overt sexual themes and content.

The Shadow of the Cat

The Shadow of the Cat

Directed by John Gilling

Produced by Jon Penington

Written by George Baxt

Starring:

André Morell as Walter Venable, Barbara Shelley as Beth Venable, William Lucas as Jacob Venable, Freda Jackson as Clara, the maid

In early 1900s England, woman is murdered by her husband and servant for her inheritance. Her cat seeks revenge.

Interesting country house set Hammer. It's something different and strange from Hammer with the cat trying to stop the murderers of his mistress.

Barbara Shelley

Barbara Shelley (1932-2021) was a British actress.

She appears in: The Shadow of the Cat (1961), The Gorgon (1964), Dracula Prince of Darkness (1966), Rasputin, the Mad Monk (1966) and Quatermass and the Pit (1967).

In Shadow of the Cat she plays Beth Venable. The Gorgon Shelley plays Carla Hoffman/Megaera. In Dracula, Prince of Darkenss she plays Helen Kent, a tourist to Karlsbad. In Rasputin the Mad Monk she plays Sonia. In Quatermass in the Pit she appears as Sonia. All of Shelley's Hammer roles were as a leading lady.

Her other roles include New Moon (1955) an Italian crime dram where she plays Amira, Cat Girl (1957) where she plays Leonora Johnson - this horror was a remake of Cat People (1942), a minor role in The Little Hut (1957), crime film The End of the Line (1957) where she plays Liliane Crawford, Postman's Knock (1962)- a British comedy film where she plays Jean, Ghost Story (1974) - a horror film where she has a minor role as Matron.

Her television work includes the miniseries Prince Regent (1979), The Borgias (1981), Blake's 7, and Doctor Who.

Shelley has been called The First Leading Lady of British Horror. She worked as a model before gaining some film roles in Italy. In later life she pursued a career as an interior decorator.

Madeline Smith

Madeline Smith (1949-) is an English actress.

She appears in: Taste the Blood of Dracula (1970), The Vampire Lovers (1970) and Frankenstein and the Monster from Hell (1974).

In Taste the Blood of Dracula Smith plays an East End Prostitute Dolly. In The Vampire Lovers she plays Emma Morton. In Frankenstein and the Monster from Hell she plays surgeon Sarah "Angel" Klauss.

Smith worked at the famous Biba boutique in her teens; the owner Barbara Hulanicki suggested that she become a model.

Other films roles include British sex comedy Some Like It Sexy (1969) where she plays Miss Beaufort-Smith. The Roddy McDowell directed Tam-Lin (1970) where she plays Sue. Up Pompeii (1971) - the film version of Frankie Howerd's Roman set comedy - where Smith plays Erotica. The Magnificent Seven Deadly Sins (1971) where she has an appearance in the Sloth segment. Carry on film Carry On Matron (1972) where she has a small role as Mrs Pullit. Famous Vincent Price horror Theatre of Blood (1973) in which she plays Rosemary. Bond film Live and Let Die (1973) where she has a memorable role as Miss Caruso.

Cliff Richard musical Take Me High (1973) where she plays Vicki. The comedy Percy's Progress (1974) in which she plays Miss UK. The Bawdy Adventures of Tom Jones (1976) - comedy in which she appears as Sophia. The Passionate Pilgrim (1983), a short film starring Eric Morecambe where she plays a Damsel.

Smith's television works includes The Persuaders, The Two Ronnies, Steptoe and Son, The End of the Pier Show, In the Looking Glass and Doctors.

Her stage credits include playing a lead role in The Mousetrap, and appearing with Alec Guinness in a West End production of Alan Bennett's play Habeas Corpus.

Spoofs

There have been numerous spoofs of parodies of Hammer horror films. This is because the film series was so long running and iconic. The nature of the films make them easy to spoof. These include:

The Carry On series made a spoof on Hammer horror with the excellent Carry On Screaming (1966).

The Kenny Everett vehicle Bloodbath at the House of Death (1983) is a spoof of horror films, including Hammer.

Dracula: Dead and Loving It (1995) is a Mel Brooks comedy with starring Leslie Neilsen. This is a parody of horror films including Hammer.

The BBC comedy show The Two Ronnies had a serial in the 1976 series called The Phantom Raspberry Blower of Old London Town which is a spoof of the Hammer horror films. It was written by Spike Milligan.

Steve Coogan made a six half an hour spoofs of Amicus, Hammer and other horror films with his 2001 BBC series Dr. Terrible's House of Horrible,. Hammer films spoofed were The Terror of the Tongs (1961) and the Karnstein Trilogy (1970–71).

T

Taste of Fear

Taste of Fear (1961)

Directed by Seth Holt

Produced by Jimmy Sangster and Michael Carreras

Written by Jimmy Sangster

Starring:

Susan Strasberg as Penny Appleby, Ronald Lewis as Bob, Ann Todd as Jane Appleby, Christopher Lee as Doctor Gerrard

Wheelchair bound Penny Appleby parents divorced when she was young. After her mother's death she lives with her father in France. Upon arrival she is told that her father is away on business and is greeted by her step mother. Later she sees her father's body in various places around the house – but no one believes her.

This is a wonderful early Hammer horror/suspense thriller. The fact that it is in black and white adds to the atmosphere. It has a great plot with many twists and an interesting cast with Susan Strasberg and Christopher Lee. Lee called it his favourite Hammer film. Taste of Fear was a big success in the UK, US and Europe.

Taste the Blood of Dracula

Taste the Blood of Dracula (1970)

Directed by Peter Sasdy

Produced by Aida Young

Written by Anthony Hinds

Starring:

Christopher Lee as Count Dracula, Geoffrey Keen as William Hargood, Gwen Watford as Martha Hargood, Linda Hayden ad Alice Hargood

In the prologue, Weller, a businessman, is travelling through the countryside in Eastern Europe. He falls off his carriage and is knocked out. When he wakes up he sees a figure with a stake through it. The figure turns to dust and Weller finds a brooch with Dracula written on it. Later, three gentleman are looking for excitement and come in contact with Dracula's servant Lord Coutley. They bring the count back to life in a ceremony involving Dracula's ring, cloak and dried blood. The gentlemen kill Courtley and the Count endeavours to get his revenge on them.

This is the fifth of Hammer's Dracula series. It follows straight on from the last Hammer Dracula film (Dracula Has Risen From the Grave (1968)). Christopher Lee return to play the Count again, and was again reluctant to do so. Vincent Price was signed up to play one of the three gentlemen, but was not cast in the end because of budget cuts to the film.

Another camp Gothic classic from Hammer with the usual production values and colourful cast. Some of the cast ham it up, but that is part of the charm!

The Terror of the Tongs

The Terror of the Tongs (1961)

Directed by Anthony Bushell

Produced by Kenneth Hyman

Written by Jimmy Sangster

Starring:

Christopher Lee as Chung King, Geoffrey Toone as Captain Jackson Sale, Yvonne Monlaur as Lee, Marne Maitland as the Beggar

In 1910, Hong Kong crime family the Red Dragon Tong murder Helena Sale to protect their identities. Captain Jackson Sale, Helen's father tries to get revenge.

This is the first Hammer horror film to give Christopher Lee the top billing.

This is a low budget, quickly made Hammer. It is great fun with cliched early 20th century Chinese villains and setting (opium dens etc). Of course it is worth watching for Christopher Lee playing the Chinese villain.

To the Devil a Daughter

To the Devil a Daughter (1976)

Directed by Peter Sykes

Produced by Roy Skeggs

Written by Chris Wicking, John Peacock and Gerald Vaughan-Hughes (based on the novel by Dennis Wheatley)

Starring:

Richard Widmark as John Verney, Christopher Lee as Father Michael Rayner, Honor Blackman as Anna Fountain, Denholm Elliott as Henry Beddows

A priest who has been excommunicated has set up a satanic cult under the guise of a Cathloic group. He persuades a man to sign over his daughter's (Nastassja

Kinski) soul to the devil. She will become the Devil's person on Earth on her 18th birthday. Her father regrets the decision and gets an occult novelist to help save her.

Dennis Wheatley did not like the film - he said it was "obscene". Natassja Kinski did a full frontal nude scene in the film, but was said to be only 15 at the time; although some say she was actually a few years older. This was the last horror film the classic Hammer studio made - before films were made with a relaunched Hammer company from 2008.

This is not the best of Hammer and a slightly dull offering. But the setting, content, interesting plot and cast make up for weaknesses in the story and a rather disappointing ending and it is very watchable. Christopher Lee is on fine form as usual as the Satanist villain.

Twins of Evil

Twins of Evil (1971)

Directed by John Hough

Produced by Michael Style and Harry Fine

Written by Tudor Gates (based on characters by Sheridan Le Fanu)

Starring:

Peter Cushing as Gustav Weil, Kathleen Byron as Katy Weil, Mary Collinson as Maria Gellhorn, Madeleine

Collinson as Frieda Gellhorn

The Gellhorn twins move in with their witch hunting strict Unlce Weil in Karnstein after they are orphaned. Frieda rebels and becomes fascinated by Count Karnstein. Karnstein is interested in Satanism and brings back Miricalla Karnstein from the grave and becomes a vampire himself.

Twins of Evil is the third in the Hammer Karnstein Trilogy. The other two films are The Vampire Lovers (1970) and Lust For a Vampire (1971). Ingrid Pitt was offered the part of Countess Mircalla, but turned it down. Unfortunately Peter Cushing's wife died just before filming started.

This is a famous Hammer horror as it features the Collinson twin sisters. This is a stylish atmospheric "Gothic sex" horror with a great plot involving twin sisters - one of whom become involved with vampirism, and the other who stays innocent. The Madeleine and Mary Collinson are extremely sexy and there is a great cast with Cushing as the very tough witch hunter, David Warbeck, Dennis Price and Isobel Black.

The Two Faces of Dr. Jekyll

The Two Faces of Dr. Jekyll (1960)

Directed by Terence Fisher

Produced by Michael Carreras

Screenplay by Wolf Mankowitz

Starring:

Paul Massie as Dr. Henry Jekyll and Mr. Edward Hyde, Dawn Addams as Kitty Jekyll, Christopher Lee as Paul Allen, David Kossoff as Dr. Littauer

Dull scientist Dr. Henry Jekyll is testing theories of alternate personalities. An experiment transforms in into another personality - Edward Hyde, a highly self confident character. As this new character he explores the darker side of London's social scene.

This is based on Strange Case of Dr Jekyll and Mr Hyde by Robert Louis Stevenson.

Another wonderful Hammer take on a famous story. There is good exploration of "the charm of evil". This has an adult tone and includes a wonderful performance by Christopher Lee as a sleazy playboy.

U

Universal Monsters

Universal Studios made a number of horror and science fiction films from the 1920s to the 1950s. In the 1930s Universal released classics such as Dracula (1931), Frankenstein (1931), The Mummy (1932), The Invisible Man (1933), Bride of Frankenstein (1935) and The Wolf Man (1941).They used "monsters" such as Frankenstein's monsters, Dracula, The Mummy and others. The films are known as Universal Monsters.

Hammer revived these monsters in the 1950s making Dracula (1958), The Curse of Frankenstein (1957). Universal Studios had worldwide distribution right for Dracula (1958), and after it was a big success Universal gave Hammer the remake rights for its Universal Monsters films.

V

Vampire Circus

Vampire Circus (1971)

Directed by Robert Young

Produced by Wilbur Stark and Michael Carreras

Screenplay by Judson Kinberg

Starring:

Adrienne Corri as Gypsy Woman, Laurence Payne as Professor Albert Müller, Thorley Walters as Peter, the Mayor of Stitl, Lynne Frederick as Dora Müller

In 19th Century Serbia, a plaque ridden village is visited by a circus .But he children in the village start to disappear.

Interesting vampire film with a selection of bizarre and creepy circus performers adding to the strange atmosphere. As this is a seventies Hammer there is extra gore and some nudity.

The Vampire Lovers

The Vampire Lovers (1970)

Directed by Roy Ward Baker

Produced by Michael Style and Harry Fine

Written by Tudor Gates (based on Carmilla by Sheridan Le Fanu)

Starring:

Ingrid Pitt as Marcilla/Carmilla/Mircalla Karnstein, Peter Cushing as General Spielsdorf, George Cole as Roger Morton, Dawn Addams as the Countess

The Countess leaves her daughter Marcilla with General Spielsdorf. Marcilla befriends the General's niece Laura who becomes ill and dies. Marcila's mother then leaves her with Mt Morton, whose daughter Emma (Madeleine Smith) also becomes ill, Vampirism is suspected in the village, and the General seeks advice of vampire hunter Baron Hartog.

This is the first film in the Hammer Karnstein Trilogy - the others are Lust for a Vampire (1971) and Twins of Evil (1972). The film was a co-production with American

International, and the last Hammer film to have American funding.

The film was more explicit than usual with nudity and a lesbian theme. The producers wanted a more adult theme to take advantage of new relaxed censorship rules.

This is a wonderful film, with the typical Hammer production values enhanced by a slightly racier tone and a great story. It has a great cast with Jon Finch and 70s glamour icon Madeleine Smith also appearing. It includes a legendary performance by Ingrid Pitt.

Mike Vickers

Mike Vickers (1940-) is a British musician.

He composed the score to Dracula A.D. 1972 (1972).

Vickers was a guitarist in the group Manfred Mann. He has arranged and composed music for numerous film, television shows and records.

W

The Witches

The Witches (1966)

Directed by Cyril Frankel

Produced by Anthony Nelson Keys

Written by Nigel Kneale (from the novel The Devil's Own by Norah Lofts)

Starring:

Joan Fontaine as Gwen Mayfield, Kay Walsh as Stephanie Bax, Alec McCowen as Alan Bax, Ann Bell as Sally Benson

A schoolteacher (Gwen Mayfield) has a nervous breakdown working in Africa. She returns to England to teach in a small town. But soon she discovers the town has a coven of witches.

Joan Fontaine bought the film rights the novel the film was based on and pitched the film idea to Hammer. Released in the Us as Th Devil's Own.

This is a reasonably good occult thriller but not a classic Hammer film. It still has wonderful English locations, and Kay Walsh has a good performance.

X

X the Unknown

X the Unknown (1956)

Directed by Leslie Norman and Joseph Losey

Produced by Anthony Hinds

Written by Jimmy Sangster

Starring:

Dean Jagger as Dr. Adam Royston, Leo McKern as "Mac" McGill, Edward Chapman as John Elliott, William Lucas as Peter Elliott

The British army are conducting radiation drills in Scotland. A radioactive entity appears leaving two soldiers burned and a deep crack in the ground. The entity returns injuring other people, and it seems to be feeding on radiation and becoming bigger.

This was going to be a sequel to The Quatermass Xperiment (1955), but Nigel Kneale did not let Hammer use the Quatermass character for the films.

This is a good science fiction horror again exploring Cold War paranoia like The Quatermass Xperiment. It has a great atmosphere - helped by the black and white film, and a great score from James Bernard.

Photo Credits

Bray Studios

https://commons.wikimedia.org/wiki/File:Bray_Film_St
udios_-_geograph.org.uk_-_1591972.jpg

8 April 2007

Chris Allen

-

Oakley Court

https://commons.wikimedia.org/wiki/File:Oakley_Court
_Windsor_2.jpg

25 July 2015

Maypm

-

https://pxhere.com/en/photo/917183

-

https://www.pexels.com/photo/grayscale-photography-
of-human-skull-1270184/

Ahmed Adly

-

https://www.pexels.com/photo/grey-concrete-ruins-under-blue-white-day-time-208308/
Pixabay

-

Bran Castle

https://www.pexels.com/photo/bran-castle-in-romania-13350095/

GirlvsGlobe86

-

Cover

https://www.pexels.com/photo/photo-of-hand-with-dark-paint-3339126/

Elīna Arāja

www.ingramcontent.com/pod-product-compliance
Lightning Source LLC
Chambersburg PA
CBHW031436130726
47989CB00003B/1164